WHEN ACTION IS NOT ENOUGH

Redefining how enterprises take strategic actions to win and find a place in a noisy world.

WHEN ACTION IS NOT ENOUGH

Redefining how enterprises take strategic actions to win and find a place in a noisy world.

AZUKA ORUMGBE

To my Mother,

Madam Janet Orumgbe whose ever loving actions God has used to help sharpen my life in every way,

And to all those who never give up thriving to lead a better life.

CONTENTS

PREFACE

Take action, take action now! You probably heard that countless times. But WHEN IS ACTION NOT ENOUGH?

Action is not enough if you cannot provide for your family

Action is not enough if you haven't achieved your goals

Action is not enough when you are yet to realize your dreams

Action is not enough if you cannot pay your bills

Action is not enough if you cannot do or go whatever you want

Action is not enough; the action is not enough....

Businesses are created to achieve massive success. But to achieve that today in a noisy world like ours goes beyond just taking mere action. It will require taking massive, incredible and strategic actions. Action that gets customers' attention regardless of incredible noise in the market place. Actions that keep CUSTOMERS much more interested and ultimately reward your business with enough revenue to keep business idea viable, sustainable and profitable. Actions that enable you to realize your dreams pay your bills and take care of your family. Achieving business and life success today requires much more than just taking action it requires a new set of attitudes, it requires new techniques and exposures necessary to create a business that impacts and keeps you positioned in any economy. **"When Action is Not Enough" is written** for this purpose; as a blueprint on how to build and grow a massively profitable business. It has become apparent that success is very predictable. There is no mystery, no magic formulae, and no alchemy. It is your attitude more than anything else that predicts your growth in business and personal life. And that is what this book hopes to expose to you.

"When Action is not enough" is a book that outlines a practical approach for business growth. It is written specifically for growing businesses; It will help businesses take a quantum leap and demonstrate how to apply ideas with excellence and originality. Turning your small business into a mega-hub requires tools, resources, and techniques that take you from just an idea into achieving incredible results.

Azuka Orumgbe

Benin.

Jan. 2020

INTRODUCTION

Action is never enough! If you think I just made this up then why not take a look at the Nigerian Micro, Small and Medium Enterprises. An ever-busy sector but never seems to add real significance to the Nigeria Economy. According to the Nigerian Bureau of Statistics, small and medium scale enterprises (SMEs) in Nigeria contribute 48% of the national GDP in the last five years, which accounts for 96% of businesses and 84% of employment. But still, the country wallows an extreme level of poverty. Check the recent report by World Data Lab (www.worldpoverty.io) Nigeria have over 95 million people living in extreme poverty that is 47.7% of Nigeria's population and they say it is rising. The country has become the poverty capital of the world. As if that is not enough it is projected that the unemployment rate for the country will reach 33.5 percent in the year 2020. That will exponentially lead to increasing crimes and criminality including murder, insurgency, armed robbery, kidnapping, drug abuse, and untold crimes. This seems to be a recurring challenge across the entire Africa continent with over 429 million people living in extreme poverty. This is quite huge and sad for a continent so blessed. Are we not taking action? Do we not work? Do we not have ideas? Did we not craft vision 2020? You see my friends; it is not just about taking action. Brain Tracy asserts that *"The high road to becoming a millionaire is starting and building your own business."* But Will that be the case for a country like Nigeria where SMEDAN and the National Bureau of Statistics asserted that the total number of MSME as of 2013 stood at over 37 million (Micro – 39 million, Small – 68, 000, and

Medium 4,670). Do these statistics show laziness, does it show Nigerians are not capable of taking action? Then how come to both poverty and unemployment rate soars every day? The answer is not action the answer is in what kind of action and how is it taken. However, we must recognize that starting and growing a business is not as easy as it sounds. Starting a business is not a facile feat. About 95% of businesses started by many Africans lacking experience fail between a month and a year. This is because many acclaimed entrepreneurs and business people know little or nothing about how to make a business successful. Only about 7% of micro-enterprises which started with less than 5 employees grow to employ 10 people or more. The question is why? Why do many African businesses hardly create brands that remain functional after the demise of the owner? For instance, Coca-Cola,

Ford, Nestlé, DuPont (1802), Citigroup(1812), Pepsi, General Electric, Procter & Gamble amongst others are still existing today even after more than 100 years of existence.

I have written **When Action is Not Enough** for this purpose; to give a blueprint on what it takes to build and grow a business. It will also help Africa's small businesses succeed and remain successful; no successful business remains small. You cannot claim to be successful and you remain small. So this book connects the dots in what seems to be the common practices that successful companies consistently carry out in other continents and clines that keep them viable even after the demise of their owner. I wrote this book to reduce the massive failure of the business across Africa and help curb the poverty and unemployment challenges in the continent.

What has become apparent is that success is very predictable; to be successful is usually fairly simple and uncomplicated. There is no mystery, no magic formulae, and no alchemy. It is your attitude more than anything else that predicts your growth even in business. Your attitude towards marketing, finance and business operations determines everything.

Action is not enough is a book that outlines a practical approach to business growth. It is written specifically for small business owners; for you to put your affairs in order and get your business to work for you. It will help you make the quantum leap and show you how to apply your ideas with excellence and originality. You need to learn to use the skills and tools to sort your business. Turning your small business into a mega-hub requires tools, resources, and techniques that take you from just an idea into taking action.

How can I get massive as a small business, HOW DO MY SMALL BUSINESS SCALE AND HAVE A VOICE IN THIS NOISY MARKET? That is exactly what this book will provide an answer for: it is a program that will transform your business almost overnight. That is not to say it is going to be easy, but it will show you that what you hope to achieve is doable.

Who should read this book?

Those who are hungry for change, those who are tired of remaining small, those who want something different for their life, those who are ready to pay the price to go beyond the limit and status quo, those who are ready to help their nations and continent experience massive lift. Although this book is specifically for a small business owner who is hungry to succeed and take their business to another level it will be of interest to all business owners whether big or small. It is written from Africa's perspective but finds relevance in any country. Many small businesses have a basic challenge; how to stay profitable and relevant. Beyond a good idea and insight, the purpose of being in business is to make a profit. Whether you work alone or employ ten or a hundred staff, the principles in this book will help you to become more effective and more profitable. You should read and reread this book if you have a passion to impact your continent positively through workable business ideas that are built to last.

Why this book was written

After a series of failures, while trying to do business, I have come to understand why a business fails. I failed because I did not know what I was doing, I was just surmising and wasting time. In this book, I am going to teach you why I once failed and almost gave up my life because I had no idea how simple it is to start and grow a business. Everything I am going to teach you is the same as I have begun to learn and apply and how I have started to experience a huge success. You too can, as all business skills are learnable.

This book is what you need to get your business going. It is a book you want to read. I have always wanted to write to help small African business owners looking for help to run better businesses. I hope it helps you take action on your ideas.

Part I

WHEN ACTION IS NOT ENOUGH

Part 1: When Action Is Not Enough

- He replied, "Because you have so little faith. Truly I tell you, if you have faith as small as a mustard seed, you can say to this mountain, 'Move from here to there,' and it will move. Nothing will be impossible for you." – Matthew 17:20 (NIV)

- "Massive action is the strategy" – Azuka Orumgbe

- "Do you want to know who you are? Don't ask. Act! Action will delineate and define you". – Thomas Jefferson.

- "The right level of action is massive Action" – Grant Cardone

- "The Path to Success Is To Take Massive, Determined Actions" – Tony Robbins

- "What we think or what we know or what we believe is, in the end, of little consequence. The only consequence is what we do" – John Ruskin

Take action, take action now! You probably heard that a couple of times. But what have you done with it? It is true action is the bedrock of creativity, and the universe will always reward action, not thought. A lot of people know this but only a few ever really act. It's our nature to want to look, analyze, maybe procrastinate and probably want to have a heavenly revelation before we ever make a move. Habitual inaction keeps us perpetually small. Many people remain small not because they do not think but because they will never take action on their thought. Don't let inaction suck out your life.

I started this book with this chapter because what I am going to share in this book is what you probably know. A lot of people already possess what they want they just fail to take necessary action to make it a reality. What you need is more action, not more knowledge. If you want to know more then take more action. Real knowledge comes from experimental action. What you know right now is already enough for you to get started on your life's vision. Taking action on your idea triggers creativity. Most of the successful people you see had no clue what they were out doing but what differentiates them from others is that they choose to take action regardless of whether they are ready or not.

One great thing about taking action is that very quickly, the universe will move once you decide to move. Resources, ideas, creativity, and finance flow to the direction of doers. Don't just talk the ideas, don't just dream the fantastic dream that makes you a fantasy; take action even though they may not be fantastic, take action even though you are labeled a fanatic, take action even if you are labeled greedy, take action even if the entire world thinks you are crazy, take action regardless of what any person thinks. The talk is cheap. Action is the currency that drives success, not mere talk. Take action on your dream; take action on your plans. There so much you could achieve if you start doing rather than talking. The world belongs to doers, not talkers. *As Sarah Ban Breathnach said "the world belongs to dreamers and the world needs doers. But above all, the world needs dreamers who do"*. Thinkers are great but do change the world because 'it is well done' is better than 'it is well said'. Abraham Lincoln did say the best way to predict the future is to create it. And creativity does not just jump on people; it comes by taking consistent massive action towards your vision until it becomes a reality.

How Massive Action Creates a Life!

Don't just take action; take massive ones. The Holy books say it best "And whoever compels you to go one mile, go with him two". If the situation of life forces you to take just one mile of action, take two. If it demands you to take two, take four. If it demands four, take eight. Have the mentality to double everything, expand everything you are given.

Take double action because one-time action never pays. You probably have heard the statement "I have tried this before, it didn't work; don't try to do it, it cannot be done." It is a common thing to be heard in our society today. People fail before they even start anything. Their failure begins from the way they think. My mum told me never to go into business for years because she felt the few times I failed proved her belief that I am not cut out for business. Was she wrong? I guess she was right at that time. I once took her advice and for years, I saw myself as a failure that could never be good in the business world. So, I started to look for a job thereby, losing time and energy. But inside of me, I was never satisfied. I knew I could not pack my bags just yet and believe what my over-protective mother thinks I am cut out to do. You see my mother gave me that advice because she was by instinct too overprotective of her little kid. She does what most mothers do. They tell their children: "play it safe, don't talk to strangers, go to school, get a job, you will never be good at this, I know what fits you, study medicine and become a doctor, go get a job with the Federal Government, I love you the way you are, I want someone by my side, there is no point working so hard, you have enough already". I was told all these things. They will get you nowhere. It is not the fault of mothers and parents that they are so protective. That is what they are wired and meant to do; to keep you from making mistakes. But following such advice will keep you in the cycle of poverty maybe forever. Mistakes and failure is a veritable tool to succeed in life. You have never experienced real failures then you may not be too ready for real success.

I am not suggesting you don't listen to counsel from your parents or guardians I am saying don't follow the counsel that will keep you small. I listen to my mother's counsel a lot but I have learned to differentiate counsel from confusion, facts from fear, advisers from adversaries, and prospect from the suspect. I have learned to be creatively deaf, I have learned to be creatively disobedient to people's counsel especially those that keep one small for long.

Do you want to create a successful life? Don't just take action, take massive action. Do something every day that beats yesterday's record. If you used to call five people in a week about your business, start calling twenty. If you used to pitch your idea to just an organization in a month, increase it to five. If you used to write for twenty minutes every day as a content writer, make it one hour. Maybe you have challenges with your relationships right now; massive action is the sure way out. If you used to call your spouse once a day, make it four times from now. Call them in the morning, once in the afternoon, once in the evening, and then maybe twice at night; your love will skyrocket. Call her when you are in the toilet, call him and tell him you are in the bathroom. Call them every time and you keep them forever thinking about you. Instead of complaining that they keep multiple partners and do not give you attention, increase the amount of time, money and energy you spend on them. If you used to buy them a gift only on their birthday, make it once a month. This also works for someone you have been trying to date but doesn't seem to have your time or probably doesn't know you exist. Increase your action; stop going home to hug your pillow thinking about them all through the night, bug them out with creative, consistent calls, show up in their salon, show up in their place of worship, be present in their social media platforms, show up in their workplace. Take this same attitude into closing all business deals. It is not just about pitching once; it is a thorough commitment to follow up until the customer makes a decision to buy and pays you for your goods or services. It is committed follow-ups until your spouse makes a decision that makes a relationship. What I am saying now is that massive action is key to living a great life.

No matter the sector you choose to operate, you can't just take a one-time action and assume you are a failure. The Holy Book says it best; "he that sowed sparingly will reap sparingly, he that sowed bountifully will reap bountifully". Don't have a 'lack' mentality when it comes to taking action. Take bountiful actions until you become an action addict.

Scarcity is a Mentality

Maybe you don't know it yet, but the scarcity mentality will cause you to not take massive actions. Take a baby, for instance, she asks daddy for a biscuit. "Daddy, I want a biscuit. Give me a biscuit". Then daddy says "you cannot have biscuit now, Janet". Now, little Janet already knows that if she wants to get the biscuit, just asking will not do it. The next line of action is, to begin with, a petty cry while still asking for the biscuit. If daddy still doesn't get it for her, then she amplifies her cries to a shout, and then to screaming, and finally to a new level of a town crier until daddy is very embarrassed and called wicked by onlookers. Unfortunately, what many parents do is to interpret and misinterpret this type of action as bad, and label the child spoilt. Some parents will even go further to scold that drive out of the child. However, what the child is expressing is the survival instinct placed in them by God to succeed in this life. Not to settle until they get what they want is a gift, not a pain, do not beat it out of them.

This kind of attitude possessed by little Janet is what you need for your life. You can't just try once or twice and give up. You need to scream and shout till the whole world, heaven and he'll hear you and get you what you want. You may not deserve it, but it doesn't matter. What matters is that you get it. Do you think Bill Gates deserves to be rich? I don't think so, but he is rich anyways. Even the Holy Scripture says "right from the days of John the Baptist until now, the kingdom of heaven suffers violence and only the violent take it by force". You cannot afford scarcity mentality in this fast-paced world, you need massive action and you need it now.

It doesn't matter whether you work for someone or you have your own business; once you commit to being a massive actionist, you get the result regardless. One man than fascinates me is Thomas Edison and how he kept taking action despite failing repeatedly. I can tell the reason you left your previous job is that the pay was not enough, right? You think so scarcely and that is why you will never get the best pay anywhere. No employer will pay what you deserve; they will renegotiate your pay. But if you take massive action that brings in undeniable profits, you will not only have them plead with you to remain with them, they will do just about anything to keep you.

Ask Dr. Ehigiamusoe, Alinko Dangote, or any successful person in your city or village; you will find that they had seasons in their lives when it appeared they were wasting their time but despite the odds, they kept pushing, praying and believing. For instance, I remember struggling with pornography for so many years; I think I am still struggling with its after effect, today. I made many commitments to myself that I just could not keep for more than thirteen years. I battled with the habit. It robbed me of my reputation, dignity, balance, progress but I kept trying. I knew that with God, the challenge would come to an end. Thank God it did! Do you want to succeed? Stop thinking like a failure. The scarcity mentality of asking at all times needs to change to the abundant mentality of giving. You can achieve an extraordinary life if you choose to. Life is the product of the actions you take today, added to the action you took yesterday and multiplied by the action you take tomorrow.

Be a scalar quantity

Let me teach you a very simple physics that will drive this home. You probably have heard about scalar and vector quantity, right? Scalar quantities are measurements that have magnitude but no direction while a vector quantity has both magnitude and direction. There is the last quantity I will like to add; VEBMO™ quantity, which has a direction but no magnitude. We, therefore, have Scalar, vector and vebmo quantities.

There is a life-transforming truth I want to point out to you. But before that, which of the quantities do you prefer? I love to be a scalar quantity first, and then a vector but I never want to be a vebmo. Young people who start life with so much energy, taking so many actions, shooting here and there and making so many mistakes and noise in the process may seem not to have a direction (scalar). Still, this is much better than being a young person who knows where they are going and have it all drawn out on paper but procrastinates on taking action.

I rather am a person who is not skillful with handling a rifle at the war front but shoots at random; I may miss my target many times but then, I will get some targets and probably stay alive for much longer than a professional shooter with the same rifle but never pulls the trigger. In business, most of us are like the 'professional shooter'. We have the skills and expertise. In essence, we have the gun but refuse to pull the trigger because of the fear of losing out. You will still die if you pull or do not pull that trigger. The earlier you pull that trigger the better your chance of staying alive. Stop waiting for the right wind. The Holy Book says "Whoever watches the wind will not plant; whoever looks at the clouds will not reap". For about 99% of the time in my life, I don't know what I am doing but I just keep firing anyway. I miss a lot of time and it frustrates me but I will continue to shoot till I hit a target. Maybe it will be a great catch, who knows? This book is one of those kinds of shots. Start with being a scalar quantity; don't wait till all conditions become perfect. Even Jesus turned water into wine before it was time for His manifestation.

A person who takes massive action without direction (even if they don't know what they doing) is far better than another who knows clearly what they ought to be doing but will never move. The reason people fall into the trap of taking no action is that they are afraid to fail.

They are afraid to be laughed at and they are afraid of losing it all. Don't let fear stop you. Don't be a vebmo quantity having direction but no magnitude. Be the scalar quantity with magnitude and no direction but tending to hit a target. Hit your target and never quit until you do. Examples of scalar quantities are speed, work, distance, temperature. Take distance, for example, once you cover enough distance at a given speed and you add time as a factor to it, it becomes velocity which is a vector quantity. Stop wasting time looking for velocity, once you cover enough distance at a speed and at a given time, you get velocity. Let's take work as another example. By the way, it is amazing that work is a scalar quantity. Once you do enough work with a force and you cover a distance while at it, it translates into a level of energy which is a vector quantity. You see, the most important elements of life do not need to have a direction to begin. It only needs to start with massive action that naturally gravitates into order.

The attitude of taking action is better than looking for what your purpose in life is. I hear people say "I want to do what I love to do", or words like "follow your passion", "pray and your angel will reveal to you what you will become in life". While I am not disputing that people can get a revelation or a premonition of what their life could turn out to be, that may not be the case for up to 90% of people. Most times, we don't need to do the things we love to do because really, not everyone loves to read, work out, sleepless, push truck or do the strenuous hustles. We only like the results of those things. I do not like too much work but I have to get doing. Nobody loves to do all these things but if you want to survive, you better do them and do them massively.

So, think scalar quantity, take more action than mere looking for direction. You have a business idea but you do not know exactly where it is heading? I bet you don't listen to people's advice, especially close family members, friends and maybe core religious individuals; otherwise, they will talk you out of it, especially if it is not a popular idea. They will advise you to give it a second thought, suggest you are not meant to do it, and even imply that the idea might not be the will of God for your life. I bet you, people will stop at nothing to keep you motionless to become valueless. Once you get an idea, take action on it no matter how small; then take incremental actions.

Another scalar quantity is the temperature it has no direction but you will not try to touch metal at 200oC. It will burn without apology. That 200OC heat can be directed to cook, roast, or can even be increased in intensity to extract valuable metals. Burn hot and burn then we can start to put order into your life and teach you what to do with your boiling youthful exuberance.

Obsession is a gift

Your obsession is not bad only that you are yet to channel it correctly. Once you begin to take action as a scalar quantity, you will become so hot that you will burn without apology. But to remain with the best ideas without taking massive action is to have the best ideas wasting. I hear people say the reason for failure is because people start too early, I tell you that you should start early. Start early, stays put and stay late. Be obsessed with your dream until you get it done.

The late Myles Moore said it best "The wealthiest place on planet earth is the cemetery. The wealthiest spot on this planet is not the diamond mines of South Africa, it's not the oil field of Iran, it is not the uranium mines of the Soviet Union, and it's not the oil wells of Iraq. The wealthiest spot of this planet is not the sea full of the ocean but the wealthiest spot on this planet is right in your neighborhood, it is the cemetery. If I could mine the cemetery as you mine gold, I will be the wealthiest man on the planet. Why is there so much treasure in the cemetery? Because buried in the cemetery are dreams that were never fulfilled, books that were never written, ideas that never became reality, and visions that were never manifested. There are in the graveyard songs that were never written. In the cemetery are great manufacturing plants that were never built and sermons that were never preached. The cemetery is pregnant with unused success. Buried in the cemetery are treasures that make God weep".

If you want to take anything to the cemetery, take massive action. Don't be a vebmo quantity. Be a scalar quantity, and then a vector quantity. Work towards doing more, not doing less. Do more! I tell you that is where the creativity is. It was the holy scriptures that asserted "But I have a baptism to undergo, and what constraint I am under until it is completed!" you must put yourself under that same constraint of massive action until you accomplish what God has deposited inside of you. Scale until you become a scalar quantity!

What I am saying is that action is a way of life and not just a choice of whether you will do something or not. Once you begin to take action, you will start seeing the best way to put your energy to work. Just the way speed with time becomes velocity; when you make enough movement early in life, you start to have direction. So, as a young person, do not allow your friends and family to tell you to rest or that you are doing too much; not even your spouse should tell you to take a break. No! Massive action releases massive output. Sure you will make mistakes but don't just fail; fail forwards, move forward with a resolve never to quit. Don't just do it once and pat yourself at the back for trying. Try again until you succeed. You will get there if you choose not to pull up or pull over. Keep moving.

Why you may have a second thought

You need to take action because, without action, you will remain potential for the best part of your life. Action is the currency for all achievements. It can be summed up in my small action mathematics as;

Potential possibility + Action = Good success

Potential Possibility + Massive action = Great Success

You are afraid of taking action for the following reasons:

1. You are afraid of failure. Up to 99% of people who never took a step to move in life were afraid of the unknown. Most times, we fear what is not real. One of the ways to move forward is to push despite your fears.

2. You don't think it is the right thing to do. Remove this cobweb from your head. Life is full of uncertainties. How are you sure you will be alive by tomorrow morning, if not for God? Take action regardless of all the 'what ifs'.

3. You think you don't have money. So you are busy telling everyone about this great idea of yours that would make you the next Bill Gates only if you could get an investor to help you with funds to kick off. *Oga*! Go sell your properties and

invest all that you have. And by the way, you don't have money problems. What you lack is the nerve to pull through on an idea. The same thing affects your relationships. Why do you think ugly and broke guys get hot girls? It is courage, my friend! They can go tell the girl about their feelings. They are not ashamed of their looks, pocket or how they might come across to the girl. They talk to her the first day, send a letter the next, and show up at her church a week after. And because they are broke, they have plenty of time to appear everywhere, funny right? They wait on her way back from work and walk her home because they know what they want. Stop looking at your pocket, look out for the bucket in your heart. The game is a massive one. It is a game of numbers. As a fact, the world is a number game, love is a number game, money is a number game, a relationship is a number game. Start from where you are.

4. You take in too much wrong data. You watch too much TV Channels and and allow your mind with many messages of fear. Boko Haram is planning to attack Kaduna, you become afraid. Militants are coming, you are afraid. Prices are going up you panic, Nigeria's economy is so bad that nothing can work here is your everyday confession; stop it! Get up, time waits for no one. Let nothing stop you from taking action today.

Action taking steps

Follow these steps to create a life of action:

Step 1: Know exactly what you want; forget the how for the moment

Step 2: Visualize the results of what you want to achieve

Step 3: Develop an emotion around the result to receive the results well when they come your way.

Step 4: Have the confidence that you can achieve whatever you set your mind on

Step 5: Who cares about gut feeling? Take a move, regardless.

Step 6: Make the move again and again, but this time, do it massively until you get the result you want.

Quotes for Chapter One

- "Be content to act, and leave the talking to others." – Baltasar Gracian
- "People may doubt what you say, but they will believe what you do." –Lewis Cass
- "Let your performance do the thinking." – Charlotte Brontë
- "Inaction breeds doubt and fear. Action breeds confidence and courage. If you want to conquer fear, do not sit home and think about it." – Dale Carnegie
- "There is only one proof of ability – action." – Marie von Ebner-Eschenbach
- "Action is a great restorer and builder of confidence. Inaction is not only the result but the cause, of fear." – Norman Vincent Peale
- "Well done is better than well said." – Benjamin Franklin

Part II

GET ATTENTION! NOT LIKING

Part 2: Get Attention! Not liking

- "Suppose one of you wants to build a tower. Won't you first sit down and estimate the cost to see if you have enough money to complete it?" – Luke 14:28 (NIV)

- "No matter how great your product or service is, no one will hear about it if you don't attract attention. It is that simple." – Sir Richard Branson, Virgin Group

- "We're here to put a dent in the universe. Otherwise, why else even be here." – Steve Jobs, Apple

- "Committed action creates consistent attention." – Azuka Orumgbe, Massive actionist, and Manufacturer

- "You can buy attention (advertising). You can beg for attention from the media (PR). You can bug people one at a time to get attention (sales). Or you can earn attention by creating something interesting and valuable and then publishing it online." – David Meerman Scott

- "Money and power follow attention; so, whoever can get the most attention is the person who takes the most action and sooner or later will get the most results." – Grant Cardone, Cardone Capital
- "90% of all success is showing up." – Grant Cardone

Attention is energy

You are either going to get attention or die in obscurity. What reason are you giving people not to forget you? You need attention to grow your business. Getting and growing attention is the number one activity every small business must be massively engaged in if it desires profitability and expansion. Potential customers must give you attention; the people working with you must know you enough to pay attention to help you build the life you deserve. The world must attend to you if you are ever going to succeed in your business. The biggest challenge for your small business right now is not money, sales, nor staff. Your biggest challenge right now is obscurity. Nobody knows you, nobody knows your business, nobody knows your goods or the services you provide, nobody knows your location, nobody knows you exist. People don't give money to strangers; you don't put money into the hands of people you don't know. I repeat for emphasis that the biggest problem in business is obscurity. You can't scale up or even scale through if nobody knows you. You can't be profitable if nobody knows you. You can never achieve profitability if you are not known. You are in the business of getting attention. The most important thing you do in business is not sales, marketing or manufacturing; it is to promote your business so people get to know you. The best product poorly promoted will sell worse than the worst product rightly promoted. Money follows attention; the more people that know you, the more money you make.

In this chapter, I will be showing you what you were never taught in school and it will help you achieve your goals and show you that by promoting your business, you stand the chance of getting attention. When to promote, how to promote, who to promote, and why it is the most important thing to do in your business is what I will cover in this chapter. If you don't promote your business; no matter how good your product or service is, no matter how good your company is, let it be free and perfect; no one will know about it. If no one knows about it, they won't buy it and if you have no person buying your product, there is no point being in business.

Liking versus knowing

There is a difference between being liked and being known. What gets attention is not people liking you. People can even hate you but still give you their attention. They may not like you or your idea but they cannot do without having to do business with you. You want to position yourself like that in business. I am talking about people knowing you and knowing what your business represents. They may not like you but still do business with you. The popularity conquest on your Facebook and Instagram page is deceptive. People get thousands of likes but are still broke. It is not about liking, it is about being known. Not everyone who likes your Facebook page is a customer. When people like your content, it is only a pointer that you have something they may be interested in but they might not know you enough to buy from you. You must be able to convert popularity into knowing. Being able to monetize your popularity is key to making it in this noisy world. When people know and trust your business, they can do business with you. The ability to convert liking to knowing is what starts the business. So, if you can use your post to make your followers on Instagram and Facebook get to know your business, purchase your product and tell their friends to buy from you; then it becomes the right vehicle. If you want serious business, you must learn not just to use social media to create awareness but also to build a business. You see those guys and girls that get the highest likes on social media platforms use their platforms to promote their brand, business or personality; they use it to get attention, not to get liked.

Wants attention? Then Promote!

The sure way out of obscurity is promotion!! You have to promote. For me, promotion comes first in this digital world of too many colors.

Promotion is part of the old five marketing mix P's:

- Product
- Price
- Place
- **Promotion**
- People

The most important "P" in that whole concept is promotion. Even if you have the best product selling for the best price or even for free and you have great potentials in people working for you as well as people who need the product; without promotion, nobody will know you exist.

We are in a very noisy world; getting attention for your business far outweighs any other marketing process.

This is how the great Apple company wizard, Steve Jobs puts it: *"To me, marketing is about values. This is a very complicated world; it is a very noisy world. And we are not going to get the chance to get people to remember much about us. No company is. So we have to be clear about what we want them to know about us."*

From that statement, we can deduce three major facts about marketing. **First, marketing is actually about value, not stories**. If you offer a product or service that makes people's lives better in some ways, you are likely to have a business. So, the bedrock is to have something to offer that people find useful; whether it is spiritual, economic, social, a material, emotional or physical value. Once your product can deliver value, you have passed the first test of promotion.

Second, you must understand that this is a very complicated and noisy world. With more than 3.8 million searches on Google per hour, more than 5 billion videos watched on YouTube every day, and more than 500 million tweets on Twitter per day; you stand almost no chance of getting known. This means no matter how valuable your product is to your market, your potential customer may never see them because of the complicated system of the world's media space. The world is too noisy and distracted to recognize what will be beneficial to them no matter how valuable it may seem.

Third, you want people to remember you and know exactly what you offer. You need to be clear about what you want the world to know about you. You want them to see that every day. Because humans are creatures of habit, it is what they see repeatedly that they can relate with. If you want to stand a chance of getting your value known in a complicated world, you need to be ready to do more than just posting randomly on social media. You need to understand the language of promotion.

The hatred game

I don't want people to always like me. I may probably want some of the hate because hatred is good for business. See how many people hated Joseph in the Bible? They even sold him to promote him. They sold him to the Ishmaelites and from there to Portifer's house. The promotion went on from there until he became the Prime Minister of Egypt. God used the hatred and wickedness directed at him to promote him to his mission in life; otherwise, he would have died a dreamer. See how many people hate and continue to hate President Donald Trump and his brand; see how many people liked Hilary Clinton. Sometimes, the negative comments of people accelerate progress. Haters are the best promoters. So, if you are the type that allows people's opinions to get to you; then you need to get a rethink. People's opinions are their opinions. Your question should be "who got my money?" If my money is in the hands of the haters, they need to give it to me and they can continue hating all they want. It will be stupid for me to think everybody will like me. Many people have publicly declared hatred for me in the past. Haters give free publicity. The more they talk, the more I get attention and the better for my business. Notice how much the Pharisees hated Jesus but how He never complained about their hatred one bit? He only rode on them and continued to go about doing good regardless of their nay sayings. However, I will never approve of how Kim Kardashian got her attention because it is a very bad example for the young generation. But you may swear and curse all you want, the lady has over 152 million cult-like followers on Instagram and it's still growing. She was the second most searched personality in the porn industry according to Pornhub 2019 report. Her fans worship her like a goddess. She has used the hatred of so many people to achieve "relevance". The people most hated are the people most empowered to be known. People will talk more about those they hate than their friends. I have heard people make snide remarks about me such as: "he is always serious, never talks to anybody, he is going to die of work, he never learns to socialize but he's always reading, he is behaving as if he knows it all, he is too fast, he pretends to be somebody when he is nobody, I don't even know what he is doing, he wants to claim all the glory here". Toxic words like these, although negative, actually are your number one promoting tool. My message is: don't always go for liking, develop content that is so good and valuable that people cannot help but just hate on you. Whether you call it jealousy, envy or badmouthing; it gives you free publicity of your brands. I, therefore, encourage you to love the haters, the naysayers, and the backbiters. Why? Because you need their promotion.

If you have not promoted your brand to an extent where people begin to complain that you are doing it too much, you are yet to start promoting. Keep promoting until people see you for who you are until the first name that pops out of their mouth when discussing fashion designing is Jane fashion and not just because you make the best clothes, but because you are the most talked about. If you are into home and office cleaning, when people mention cleaning services, let your name be the only thing in their mouth. You are doing something but it is not enough; you need to promote your business to build an audience. People don't buy from who they like but who they know. Do you want to be known? Do you want to keep being known? You have to learn how to promote.

You can't be scared and get money at the same time. One thing my mum taught me is not to save money in a bank. Once you make money, put it back into the business or use it to develop another stream of income. She taught me consistency; keep doing a thing until everybody knows you and pays you. I am grateful for that training. She spends money in her business, she outspends everybody. She invests so much in getting her business moving until it starts yielding profit. We live on a planet where things happen so fast and there are so many reports that prove playing safe in one little corner will suck the life out of anything. Doing it massively until you get attention is the key ingredient to get out of obscurity. Keep putting your business, product, contents out there because people will forget about you real soon if you don't. Consistency is the way to greatness. If you want to succeed in business and life, you have to get known. Not just being liked, but getting known. The more people know you, the more the resources that flow to you.

How to get attention

Be willing to go knock on doors

attention requires you to know how to knock on doors. You cannot negotiate that off; you need to be in people's faces every time. Your ability to knock on doors is where expansion starts. Sales are how you get attention, sales are what ensure you do not starve, sales help you take care of your family, sales is what makes your dreams a reality. You need to keep prospecting, making presentations, handling objections, closing sales and getting resale and referrals. You need to keep on being in people's face screaming 'who got my money?' Getting attention is more than one Facebook post or Instagram video. You must be ready to sell. You cannot focus on saving at the expense of growing your business. You should invest in making your business known at all times.

To get the attention you need to know how to sell because you cannot grow a business without a proper sales sense. Were you brought up not to talk to strangers and be seen but not heard? If you want attention, you must learn to do the opposite. You must learn to talk to a stranger and you must be seen every day and heard every time. Attention equals profitability. You cannot afford to wait for customers to come to knock on your door; you need to go find them like a lost treasure. You need to search them out from their holes of complaints about how bad the economy is, low funds, and a tight budget. You need skills to achieve this? (***Call Azuka Dery on +2348068387128 to get you and your company trained on making sales so easy, and profitability so high).*** You can't grow a business in obscurity. Get attention. Be massive in your approach and save yourself and your family from financial embarrassment.

You need frequency

attention requires a lot of frequency. You need to keep putting your message out there until somebody calls you for business. Another name for frequency is committed consistency. You need to stay committed to your promotional activities until you get the attention of your target market. Many small business owners with great ideas die out fast because they promote their business three to four times, maybe seven times and give up. Studies show that it takes seven to ten presentations for someone to make up their mind to take any form of action. It is a shame to take one or two promotional actions and give up with the excuse that you have tried. You need to be willing to take promotion action over and over again until people take action to buy from you. Consistency is the key ingredient to getting attention in today's noisy world.

Be willing to show up

Show up every day regardless of how you feel or whether it is time or not. Show up regardless of whether the environmental condition is perfect or not; in rain or the sunshine, show up. It is better to be the available lamb than to be the dead lion in any jungle. Show up in your customers' email, their Instagram page,

Facebook page, and YouTube channels. Show up in their house, club, and for their social event. Show up on billboards, radio, and TV. Show up in their churches, mosque and everywhere your customers present themselves. You must commit to showing up to get attention. You want to get attention, show up!

Be ready to over-commit and over-deliver

just commit; commit more than you can keep. It will help you stress and think about other options to explore. Commit and figure out the rest later but first, make commitments. A customer tells you to deliver on a certain date; tell them you will deliver two days earlier and make a commitment to pull through. A customer tells you to provide a certain service; add more to it and make it free for them. Then, deliver value beyond what you are paid for. That is a sure way to get attention. Go beyond your customers' expectations. Blow their minds with quality, quantity and timely delivered goods and services.

Be your unique self

Be yourself, be unique and don't be a copycat. Be the original version of yourself. Sell products, deliver services that make you stand out. Customers will never reward you for your similarities but your differences. Be different from the rest. Even if you are into the commodity business, look for strategic business advantage in your packaging. Don't just be a best practice person. By that, I mean don't just do well what everyone does. Have a unique competitive advantage; something that makes your customers perceives that difference in what you offer. Two people can be into the restaurant business but one is more popular than the other. Most times, it won't be because the more popular a person's food tastes better but because they have found a way to package the business better; either in food delivery services or a special feeling they give to their customers that makes them to continually sing the praise of that business.

Use all available media

Hear people say I am a Facebook person or I am a WhatsApp person; that is funny. You must go where your customers are to get their attention. If they are in the bush, you need to go meet them there. It is not about what you want; it is about what they want. As a small business owner, it is not expected that the entire world becomes your market. You must need to position your business to the market that needs it to save resources. Once you know your target niche, you must build your promotion around that niche to get the attention of your customers. For instance, assume you are into the cleaning business; you must first identify which demographics need your services. So, let's say your target would be single, high-class working guys between the ages of 27 and 55 who are usually too busy to do a detailed cleaning of their homes. Then, you discover they live in places like GRA in Benin City, and their more preferred social media platform is Facebook and Twitter. What most business people do is to focus on Facebook promotions only and ignore other portals. If these guys are of these demographics, it means you could get their attention not just from Facebook but from other sources. You need to find a way to reach them also on Twitter and do a personal visit to their homes and places of worship. You need to cover up all the space these guys are found in. Don't focus on one channel and leave the other channels underutilized; you might be making a grave mistake. Anywhere and everywhere your potential customers can be found in the place you want to promote your brand. Getting attention requires spreading your tentacle towards a focused market group until they know you exist and buy your business. If they don't know you, they will not buy from you. If they don't buy from you, then you are not in business.

Create inventories

The number one reason businesses fail is the inability to sell products in quantities great enough and margin high enough. Don't just sell one thing; have a range of product lines and service lines to present to your customers. That is why you need to master the science and art of selling. Customers do not want this line of product you are presently offering right? You should have another product at hand close to that other product. By this, I don't mean for you to be the jack of all trades. I mean have inventories in relationship to what your business covers. Back to the cleaning business as an example, if you are into cleaning, you should create a range of services from full apartment cleaning to window cleaning, doors cleaning, and tiles cleaning. Come out with a service that will be most needful, convenient and affordable to the customer per time. In essence, if a customer tells you they cannot afford a full apartment cleaning; you could offer them the window cleaning service, and if they aren't satisfied with that, you could present to them the offer of tiles cleaning. If they still wouldn't take that offer, you could suggest selling them a cleaning product they would use to clean at their convenience. That way, your customers can in one way or the other buy your product or service and keep you in mind for subsequent purchase. You know the saying that the first purchase is the hardest. Once a customer buys anything from you no matter how small it seems, you have open a whole window of future bigger purchases. So offering multiple lines of options for your customers to choose from is not just an option for small business owners but a necessity. Don't just offer one product; have a range of product offerings.

Be flexible

must be flexible in dealing with your potential customers to get their attention. This, however, does not mean you should lose control over your business. You must be ready to offer customers a range of services on flexible terms and price range. If for instance, you come up with the idea of making free solar power panel installations at subscription prices, you should be able to cater for every customer by their purchasing capability such that, from the least paying customer to the highest paying customers, they all should be able to use your service and be able to pause and resume that service as preferred. Such a level of flexibility will promote trust for your business and help you get attention if there are competitors.

Major on the majors, not minors

Everyone is your market. Focus on the major, not the minors. Once you establish a particular market niche, focus on that niche until you get the attention of every potential paying customer in that niche. What niche marketing does is that it helps you tailor your services to a particular group of a segmented market that needs your product and services and also helps you satisfy, monitor and evaluate their needs in definite ways as compared to spreading your tentacles everywhere. A good example will be the Auto Industry. Maserati and Ferraris are not marketed to the entire customer populace but to a specific, targeted audience that has the financial capability to buy. Those brands of cars are therefore not produced in mass because they don't need to be available in car dealerships like others. It is easy to get the attention of a niche than to focus on the entire world. Promotion tailored to a niche will get more attention than the general advertisement. If you are in the cleaning business, for instance, you must know that not every person needs your service. People who are likely to be interested in your service would be working-class people who have a level of income that can pay for the service and who live in a specific area. Going to market your service on TV may likely be a wasted investment because they are hardly available to turn on their TVs. Even if the TV were an option, your promotional message must be aired at a targeted time, and with the right appeal to get their attention. Understanding who you serve and how best to send your promotional appeal is the sure way to get attention.

Commit to being the light

The light that shines in dark places. Let the customer see how brightly you can shine by exceeding their expectations. Your business idea must be valuable as light is of great value in darkness. One major characteristic of bright blazing light is that it cannot be hidden. You try to hide it in darkness, it will be seen. When the light comes on, darkness finds its way out. So, in this noisy world to go above the noise is to let your business be a bright and shining light. Let your idea, business, service so deliver value that you become irresistible. Amazon, Google, Walmart, and Dangote Group are organizations that have lighted up our world and the world cannot but flow in their direction. But the concept is not just about light, otherwise, we can also classify candlelight as light even though it could easily be put out by a mouth full of breath. The power of light depends on how much of darkness it can disperse. In other words, the value of your business is dependent on how much attention it can garner. Light is always a function of its intensity and how that light is positioned in its stand. To promote, you must be a source of illumination, shining so brightly that you cannot be ignored. There are two main concepts of light your small business can apply;

- The *Illuminating Capacity*, and
- The **positionin**g of the business

Illumination capacity refers to the **inherent attractiveness** of the business in that industry for profitability. Every business can only succeed in the long run if it possesses some kind of superior capabilities to succeed in a given industry. The capacity to illuminate adequately as a business person is what guarantees business success both for the short and long term. The illuminating capacity of a business, therefore, begins with taking a critical look at the entire business, the potential of the industry it operates, the product or service's capability to meet the need of potential customers, and the sustainability of the idea. *See Michael porter five forces for a thorough understanding of business attractiveness.*

- **of the business** refers to how to achieve superior performance. You can be different by commanding a higher price because you have a product or service that the customer is willing to pay more for. Still a good example is the Auto Industry mentioned earlier. They sell high ended cars at higher prices but serve smaller margin of the market; this is referred to as cost leadership. Positioning could also be that you have a lower price because you can serve a greater quantity of the market based on the economics of scale. An example is Spanx, a company that produces pantyhose for females. Who exactly you are trying to reach and how you reach them is what is covered doing industry analysis.

Use the right vehicle

You have developed your content and inventories and now need to put that content in the right vehicle to reach the target market segment. Which is the best vehicle? Is it the Media houses (Television, radio or print media), digital space (website, blog or social media platforms), telephone calls, or door to door marketing? Any vehicle you wish to employ to deliver your content must be the right vehicle. The right vehicle is the vehicle your customer is in. You must find where your potential customers are always going to get information and put your promotion activities there. For example, assume you sell anti-aging products and your target market are men and women between the ages of 65 and 79 years; it is very unlikely that this class of people will use the internet or look at billboards to get information for their need. They probably are still stuck to the old conventional print media such as newspapers, circulars, and magazines. That is their vehicle. Armed with this knowledge, promoting your business on Instagram for such a target market becomes an abuse of time, money and energy. It is like taking the wrong bus while traveling at night, it can be very frustrating. You may get lots of likes on that platform but that does not mean that platform will deliver good results. First, they may like the product but they do not need it at their age since Instagram is predominantly a vehicle for the young. Second, even if they do need it, they may not have the financial capacity to pay for it. You now know that being in the right vehicle is a must to get attention for your business. You, therefore, have to understand your market demographics properly for you to put your content in the right vehicle. Not all promotions get attention even when liked. Without attention, people won't know you and if they don't know you they will not buy your products.

More on developing contents to get attention

As part of thinking massively, I am adding this section to dwell more on the benefits of developing more content for your business. To get the attention you will need more content, and you will need to know how to sell using the right vehicle. You need to master the art of developing content. By that, I don't mean your content has to be so great and professional; otherwise, you will spend much time deliberating on content at the detriment of other responsibilities. Still, you need content, enough content that will make people know you.

Benefits of developing more content

- It helps you think differently for different sections of your business.
- It ensures you target different sessions of the market.
- It helps you develop content faster for each service category.
- It pushes you to have varieties to show your customer so if they cannot afford a

product or service, they could opt for a cheaper and similar one.

- It brings dynamism to your business. You always have something to share with different market segments.

- It makes you creative; you are never bereft of ideas for content.

Prerequisites to develop more content

To increase the volume of content you develop, you need:

- Frequency
- Staying muscles
- Promotion skills
- Marketing and sales skills (sales cycle and business cycle)
- Negotiation skills
- Digital skills
- Dynamism
- Networking skills, and
- Massive thinking

Steps to help you take action

1. What are you currently doing to get attention for your business?

2. Do you have a strategy to promote your business?

3. Write out fourteen promotion ideas you can use to get attention for your business.

4. Write out seven other means you could take to get your products out there.

5. Take time to study how successful businesses around you promote their business, apply the same strategies for your business.

6. Re-read this section until you fully understand the entire concept.

7. Call Dery today to get your organization trained on how to do profitable social media promotions (call Dery on 08068387128).

Part III

DOMINATE OR COMPETE, WHICH WAY?

Part 3: Dominate or Compete: Which Way?

- "And God said; let us make man in our image, after our likeness: and let them have dominion over the fish of the sea, and over the fowl of the air, and every creeping thing...." Genesis 1:26 (NIV)

- "There is not healthy competition" – Azuka Orumgbe

- "When I step onto the court. I am ready to play. If you are going up against me, you'd better be ready. If you're not going to compete, I will dominate you." – Micheal Jordan

- "You will always fall to the level of your training. Are you here for fun, to compete, to win or to dominate?" – Matt Danswan

- "The only way to dominate in an industry is to find a way to add more value to other

people's lives than anyone else is adding."
– Tony Robbins

- "Never make it a goal to compete; instead, do everything you can do to dominate your sector to avoid spending your time chasing someone else." – Grant Cardone

Domination, not competition is the game. To compete is to make an earnest effort for superiority or victory over another, a kind of contention, contest or even conquest over a scarce or limited resource. To dominate, on the other hand, is to have supremacy, mastery, the ruling power, hegemony or controlling influence over a thing. Which do you prefer? The great management guru, Peter Drunker, and the erudite marketing geniuses, Michael Porter and Philip Kotler wrote extensively on competition and how to compete. They believed that having a competitive advantage enables a business to win in any market space. They compared business to fighting a war, where you need to fight so hard to win. While that might seem to sound good, I recommend that you quit thinking that way, if you are ever going to find a foothold in today's economy. Quit thinking of competitive advantage when your business could become a force to reckon with. What it takes, how it could be achieved and how to sustain domination is what this chapter is all about.

Compete or dominate

I am a fan of strategy. I belong to the school of thought that as a business owner, you need to understand your business's industry, know its position in that industry, know the exact audience and market it is supposed to serve, and have the strategy to be visible enough to command a level of market share in that industry. But still, I am no fan of competition.

Why compete when you can dominate? The money is in domination, not in competition. Domination is the central focus of any serious-minded entrepreneur. All successful business people do not compete. Bill gate, Elon Musk, Jeff Bezos, Sarah Blakely, Mark Zukerberg, Aliko Dangote, and a host of many others. Successful businesses people know that competition is for mediocre and more suited for average people who are queuing up for limited resources and so have to fight to get ahead. Rather, they opt to dominate in the market effort, then, market share and ultimately in the overall revenue of the industry they belong to.

We must recognize that as humans, we are not wired to compete, but dominate. It is lower animals that compete. Human beings were created to dominate and subdue the elements of the earth. So, no matter the industry you belong to, you must have the mind of a dominator and not that of a competitor. In the free enterprise economy, while monopoly may not be an ethical ideal, companies now overshadow competitors by out-promoting their brands to the market. Superior revenue helps them to do superior market research which again helps them to develop the best products. Because they do good market research and have the best of products together with the ability to out-promote, they dominate naturally. How do you compete as a small business owner, with massive brands like P&G, Unilever, or Dangote group? It is foolhardy to compete with those that have massive resources, network, experience, and reach when all you have is your small business which has just started with little or nothing but an idea.

Competitive or Dominating advantage

The idea of competitive advantage may sound good to many people but I prefer you have a dominating advantage; something unique that only your business can offer. Once you have a unique set of value propositions that cannot be copied and you can promote it creatively in such a way that the entire market recognizes you as the only one who offers this product and repeatedly buys from you, you are no longer competing but dominating. This is what Sarah Blakely is doing with Spanx. Sarah Blakely is a billionaire in the fashion and clothing industry not because she has monopolized the market but because she found a need that her idea can meet and she explored it creatively so that females are now grateful for the product which has been able to consistently solve their cater for their need. Spanx never competed with any clothing line but dominated her found niche.

The difference between a dominator and a competitor can be likened to the current of the ocean where you are either swimming with the current or creating the current. No swimmer swims against the mighty current of the ocean if they want to survive. So what a skillful swimmer will do is to let the ocean current drive them effortlessly to their destination. But to be a dominator, you need not follow the tides or rules. Rather, you need to create your current, do your thing, and follow your rules. While it may not be bad to let an existing current drive you effortlessly to your destination, I recommend that to succeed in this new digitalized social media economy, you need to generate your current which you can control, adjust to fit your purpose, and own. That is exactly what Jeff Bezos of Amazon did to create one of the most valuable businesses today. He had an idea, grew the idea and made sure the idea became a global relevance. Dr. Ehigiamusoe did the same. He started a lending business with just 100 nairas at Delta State, Nigeria. He has since built a massive lending business, creating a mighty current. Today, Lapo organizations employ more than 7,000 Nigerians and many others across Africa with multiple products, services and value to Africa and beyond. The man is not competing, he is dominating. Don't compete, dominate instead. Create your current and make your idea stick so well that in your industry, it is only your name that is known when they mention the type of service or product you offer. Be the king of the jungle.

The product that has the highest frequency and appears consistent in adverts always out-compete any competitor in that field. You may not have the advert budget of a big company but as a small company, you can promote to dominate with the platforms available to you. Why compete when most people will never do more than the status quo. Domination, not competition is the way small businesses remain relevant in their industry.

How to dominate your space

Begin with yourself

Domination, unlike competing, does not require analyzing the externals. Domination starts with you and not from the externals; so, stop looking at the outside environment. Your first need is not a Michael Portal industry analysis model. You don't need the value chain concept; neither do you need the mamba analysis. What you need is an internal evaluation of who you are and what you want to achieve. What do you want? Know that real domination is not about dominating people. It is equally not about market domination first. Real domination starts from one's self, you! What you stand for, your value, ethics, your obsession, your purpose, your capacity, your integrity, what you represent, your drive, your ability never to give up, and your resolve to succeed; all of these make up your internal dynamics.

Steven Covey asserted "inner victory precedes public victories". It is internal domination before external domination. The concept of domination is not entirely new. In the Holy Scriptures, God commanded man to dominate, not to dominate another man but to dominate the earth; and the earth of every man is figuratively the internal world of that man. To prove this, we will need to look at a statement in the Holy Book. Jesus, while speaking in a parable said "the kingdom of heaven is like a grain of seed that a sower sowed"; describing the ground into which the seed was sown as the heart of man. Some other verses in the scriptures also talked about cultivating the heart. Now, the only place where we cultivate is the earth's land. This earth therefore metaphorically describes the internal dynamics of a man. Man is meant to first dominate the earth that is his mind, not other people. This means your domination should not be domination over fellow humans but **self-discovery, self-mastery, and self-fulfillment**. Once you master yourself, your emotions, your reaction, and your responses; you become the master of your earth, your world, and your globe.

Self-discovery

You abuse a thing you do not know its value. A life is abused when it is without a purpose. Most people go through life each day without actually living because, for the most time, they do not know why and what they are meant to do. To dominate, you must first search diligently for why you are here and what you are meant to do; something that keeps you awake every day, something far bigger than you, and something that keeps you fired up. Finding requires a search. You need to do an inner search for the reason for your existence. Every human being has a purpose; only that many never discover it. You hear a lot about suicide these days because, without a mission and life's objectives, depression is bound to set in. If you have a real job to do, you will never be depressed. If you have a purpose so compelling that it keeps fueling your energy, you will want to find out how you can make it a reality.

To find your life's purpose, you should ask yourself these questions;

- What do I want from life?
- How long do I intend to be here?

- What do I like doing?
- What do I do repeatedly?
- What do I enjoy doing such that even if nobody pays me, I will still do it with all my heart?
- What turns me on when I see other people do?
- What do other people praise me for that I do not see as work?
- What kind of things do I enjoy doing, and do effortlessly?
- What keeps me awake at night?

Use these questions to probe into your purpose in life. Lastly, you should go ask your creator. Every product manufacturer knows the intent, design, and use of any product they make. We, humans, have a manufacturer and that is God. Knowing that, it is only wise to go into a concerted search, and prayers for Him to guide you into your life's purpose. Some people will argue this either because they are atheists or because they think they are self-sufficient. Well, no one is self-sufficient; not even the devil. Just try it out to avoid doing what is meant for someone else to do. This will ensure you are not merely running a rat race and competing. There is something God created you for, there is an idea you can conceive. The reason many people compete is that they have refused to be humble enough to acknowledge the supremacy of God in their life. If you want to dominate, then go find your purpose. That is where it starts.

Self-mastery

It is the lack of self-mastery that leads to life's misery. Once you discover your purpose, you need to master yourself as you drive towards that purpose. To dominate, you must master self and it involves asking the following questions:

- How knowledgeable am I about what I hope to achieve?
- Do I have the necessary skills needed for what I want to achieve?
- Am I ready to put in the necessary work to achieve my life's purpose?
- Am I ready to delay gratification until I achieve my aim?
- Am I ready to go the extra mile to achieve this my life's purpose?
- Am I ready to get up and try again no matter how many times I fail?
- Am I disciplined enough to wake up before anyone else?
- Am I ready to sacrifice my comfort, meals, sleep, and all I care about, to achieve my purpose?
- Am I ready to be stressed until I get the work done?

- Am I ready to do whatever it takes to achieve my purpose?

Self-fulfillment

You must come to a point in your life where you are not satisfied until you get the work done. Until you get to the point where you know you have finished the course, won the race and got the crown, you must learn never to give up. Don't give up until you become fulfilled and have achieved your benchmark. The inner peace of achieving a set purpose makes you a dominator and helps you think like one in every area of your life.

Possibility is positive

The number one reason for competition is limited resources. Often, resources are limited; therefore, people tend to compete for the scarce resources available. One thing you want to start doing is to begin to think differently. If you think about scarcity like others do, things are going to get scarce all around you; your profit will be scarce, good people will be scarce around you, even your happiness will be scarce too. Still, if you think of lack always, you are going to experience it. Put simply, you are going to be behind if you think too small. As it is often said, you cannot solve problems with the same level of thinking that created them. So, stop thinking competition, think domination! Stop thinking about limited resources, think abundance! Think big, and think massive! Whatever industry you are in, whether you are an employer or an employee, you need to think like a dominator or a terminator or better still a bulldozer. For instance, if you make bread, you need to first get your internal dynamics right. After that, you are now to think as big as how your bread business can feed the entire Africa continent instead of thinking about how your fellow bread makers are faring. The scriptures affirm that as a man thinks in his heart, so he is. We are what we repeatedly think, it's that simple. The way you think determines who you are. As food builds the body, so does the thought shapes the mind. You are who and what you constantly think. Want to dominate? Change the way you think. Think dominating thoughts, think winning thoughts. Do you remember Adolf Hitler, the man who wanted to conquer the world? Thinking about one of my favorite Bible stories, the story of David and Goliath; where the tiny teenager David faced the giant Goliath without fear. The truth is, David had the mind of a giant even though he had a small body. With such mind, he was able to bring down the giant despite how big he was. That you are a small business does not mean you cannot dominate in the market place. To achieve such a feat, you need to change the way you think. You probably are thinking too small. You see yourself as the Israelites saw themselves before the Nephilim (the descendants of Anak). They saw themselves as grasshoppers and equally taught that was how the people saw them. You are what you think.

To dominate, you must remove the 'grasshopper mentality' from your head and see yourself as a giant able to dare other giants that are probably an illusion. The giant of fear concerning funding, available market, or product acceptance, the giant of procrastination and every other giant that wants to stop you from making a move are mere illusions in your mind, no matter how real they seem. Face your fears, raise your thinking, raise your game and go dominate your sphere.

Thinking about the possibility of failure is the first step towards remaining under slavery.

Once you face your fears and stop letting your small thoughts dominate your action, you dominate your business sphere and build an incredible business. Change the way you think about your business and your life. Changing your thinking requires getting new data.

A deliberate decision to replace your source of information is what determines if your thinking will change. The term information simply means ideas (data) that form. The info you get and the data you input into your mind can influence the way you think. You, therefore, need to choose to change the things you watch, listen to as well as what you allow your five senses to pick up. Some of these things may be outrightly poisonous to your mind. You can't be addicted to pornography for instance, and expect to be a successful business person. As I mentioned much earlier, I used to watch a lot of pornography and it affected my thinking. I viewed life so bizarrely and saw girls as an object to be toyed with, so I basically could not keep any friends. It was so bad I could not have a business discussion with a female because I would get myself all messed up while undressing them in my mind even if they were clients that meant well for my business. I developed low self-esteem and would crawl into my little corner whenever I experienced failure. Even when I experienced some degree of success, I was back in the same cycle of regret. So any dead-end habits fueled by the wrong data need to be stopped. Stop fueling your passion with bad fuels. Bad fuels like excessive use of drugs, alcohol, and porn will ruin your chance at a successful business. You need to control the data you input into your mind.

Some information pushes the mind to fear, depression, stagnation, and disinterest; they sap the energy out of your soul. While such information can be easily identified and avoided, some subtle ones are capable of keeping you small for a very long time. These kinds of information which may be a piece of news aired at a point in time, a terrorist group invading a certain area, a bigoted comment or even pieces of poor advice from parents, spouses or religious leaders; must never be accepted or allowed on your mind.

How to think differently

Look for information that will shape your life and give you the resilience to win in the game of life. What creative unlimited thinking does is that it pushes you to see from a different horizon. It forces you to think around and outside the box. To achieve what I am talking about, I recommend the following steps to help you kick start a new way of thinking:

First, go to the universe. You must agree with what Sarah Blakely calls the universe. That there is for sure a higher power that controls or sets a balance for the human race. You can't assume the universe is a freak of occurrence. Someone or something must have set it up. On my part, I recommend you read the Bible and take it as number one source of new data and info. Regular reading of the scriptures has been proven to reduce stress by 33% and reduce the propensity to view pornographic material by 70%. Also, it can relax the mind. While other religious books could help, reading the Bible has worked and keeps working for me and millions of others.

Second, invest time and money to study at least a book that is related to your field per month. It helps you to know your industry and come out with new ideas.

Third, get a life coach or a mentor to spend time with. Don't make the mistake of having multiple mentors at a time. That is one trap many people get into. Pick one and do a detailed study of their life. If your coach or mentor is far from your location, you will need to immerse yourself in their materials such as books, videos, and online classes.

Fourth, study at least one global business outside your industry. It will broaden your horizons.

Fifth, Attend conferences and seminars.

Sixth, listen to audio and video programs on the internet as it relates to your field and motivation.

Seventh, watch the company of friends you keep.

Eight, turn off the television for certain hours of the day

Ninth, stop unnecessary activities that will never help you realize your goal in life. Incessant partying is a part of these activities.

Tenth, stop following the crowd; dare to be different.

You could choose to do many different things, but you must know that whatever informs your sense organ influences your sense of judgment. If you need to be influenced by anything, let it be productive and creative things that pull you towards your goals rather than away from them.

Get your money mindset right

People who think too small of themselves will always have trouble with their finances. Money has never been the root of all evil otherwise; you will label all our religious leaders evil. A wealthy individual comes to your church and donates a million naira; you then see how many people jump, celebrate and forget why and what they came to do in church. Usually, money brings happiness, the more money you have the happier you are likely to be. Money by itself isn't evil. Rather, it is the worship of money that is evil. You need money to live a good life; life will be evil without money either in the bank, real estate or in other assets. Many people have the wrong mentality about money and that is why they remain poor for a long time. The way you think about money matters a lot because it shows whether you will attract or repel it. You can forget about ever being rich if you are fond of thinking and making statements like "money will not make me happy; I am better just as I am; big man, big trouble; I am satisfied with my financial level, I don't need more, I am contented with what I have and what I am (how can you be contented with poverty?), money is the root of evil; life is not all about money;

money cannot buy happiness". Of course, money cannot do everything, but it is obvious that you need money to enjoy life. You cannot change the state of a person if the knowledge they have about money is wrong. One of the ways I tell you have a negative mindset about money is the way you talk. Your mindset shows in your words. When you make out liabilities to be assets and vice versa, it shows you have a negative mindset about money. If you want to have the correct money mindset, you need to know and speak the money language. You need a correct definition of:

- Assets
- Liabilities
- Revenue
- Profit and loss
- Income statement
- Cash flow
- Return on investment (ROI)

- Equity
- Variable margin rate
- Hard work, and
- Luck

The basic financial terms listed above are what you need to understand to change what and how you think about money. How you think about money will influence what comes in for you. Money is like a magnet; the more you create an environment for it, the more it finds access to you. When I talk about money, I don't mean the paper printed by the Central Bank now and then, but the entire legal tender; the paper and non- paper assets. The distance between you and money is a problem you should be willing to solve. An average African today, is satisfied with the status quo which is either to go to school or learn a trade, then make enough money to take care of their family, build a house or two, buy a couple of cars and retire at old age. That is the blueprint people often navigate with but who says there can't be more? People who think too small of themselves will always have trouble with their finances. The way you think about money is the way you use it. If you have 'scarcity thoughts', a *give me-give me* kind of mentality, you are liable to be perpetually broke. Money in the hand of a great user will be used to generate profitability to help build industries that will create lots of jobs thereby creating happiness for many people. Someone made a very interesting comment about money when they said: "money is like oxygen". You do not worship oxygen but you need it to stay alive. In the same vein, you do not worship money but you need it to stay alive; you need it to legally transact life deals.

To know how to use money, you need a good money mindset. You need to believe that money in itself is not evil, and that you deserve an abundance of it. You need to know that there is so much money on the planet and that you have some of it will in no way diminish the amount available to others. You need to ask 'who got my money', know how to get it from them, and also know how to adequately utilize it to create a great life for yourself as well as help solve others' problems. Money is a defense against poverty, embarrassment, frustration and even untimely death. The ransom of a man's life is indeed his riches.

The principle of money

"Money doesn't grow on trees; you should save in the bank; you need money to make money; spend a little of your earnings, save the rest to become rich" are probably the things you heard and learned while growing up. Those kinds of financial advice do not work anymore.

Compounding is the way to wealth. Putting your money in the bank with a 0.2% rate will never make you rich; not in the next 100 years. However, knowing how to invest that money in yourself, then your business and subsequently in other people's business with good returns is the key to building wealth. Dominating in the market place requires that you know how to generate money and invest such money to get more. The more revenue you get from your business, the better you dominate. Understand that domination entails producing enough profit for your business to invest it to promote yourself and your brand and out-research anyone in your business.

The use of money

There are three things you do with money; one, you go get it, two, you keep the money with the intention to invest and not to save, and third, you put it into something that produces more money. I cannot over-emphasize the need to invest in yourself first, then your business, the people that work with you, and then in assets. Invest in businesses that do not easily get disrupted; food production, water supply, and housing are businesses that do not easily get disrupted even with technological changes.

How to develop a correct money mindset

One, change your sources of information. Be more concerned with information that tells you about abundance, not scarcity.

Two, connect with the right people. Be with people that help you think correctly about money and those who go-ahead to take actions that generate money. Don't join the group of mere talkers; join the group of people who take actions that have yielded visible positive results. In other words, connect with people who match their words with action or who do not talk much but do a lot of stuff that is evident.

Three, change your environment. Go to places that inspire you to take financial action. If you need to travel, do. If you need to visit somewhere better than your environment, please do. Most times, we are caged into thinking so small financially because of the kind of environment we live in. If you live in a village with mud houses everywhere, where your music comes from birds and the best occupation around is subsistence farming; you are going to think small. You will probably also build a mud house, maybe reinforced with cement blocks and will never hear the sound of pop, Rand B, and other good music in your lifetime, unless you leave that environment. Changing your environment is changing your financial mentality.

Fourth, read, study, listen and watch. The greatest education is that of the mind done outside the walls of a classroom. Read books about finances, study people and study businesses. Study materials until you can impress on yourself a different and positive kind of thinking about money. Nobody will teach you all there is to know about money but as you take time to study books, people and business, you will begin to create a different mindset about finances and identify where to invest to get maximum returns.

Fifth, be disciplined about spending. Create a mental blueprint on how you should spend your money and configure your life that way till you make it happen. Someone can spend ten years making money but blow it away in ten days. That is where reading and studying becomes important. When you read, your mind becomes informed well enough about how money is meant to be spent. That way, when you make money, you will know where to put it such that more will flow in. People are spendthrifts because they lack the knowledge of how to make money work for them. Being disciplined enough about money boils down to the way you think. If you think that money is meant to be lavishly spent, you will always squander it whenever you make it. What you think about money and how you spend it determines your financial freedom to a large extent.

Have a clear cut goal

Clarity precedes confidence. The clearer you are about a matter, the more confident you become. Once you are clear about what you want to achieve, it is as good as fifty percent complete. Once you have a target, don't lower that target; rather, increase the activities. As soon as you clearly outline your plan and correctly map out a space for your life, it becomes easy to dominate any field you set to explore. You may not know the entire way; you may not even know the eventual destination but so long you are clear about what you want, the rest becomes history. To be clear, you need to have a practical understanding of your mission in life and must be able to answer why and how to achieve what you hope to achieve. Domination won't come until you are clear on what you want.

Define your field and take massive action

You are not meant to be everywhere doing everything because you are not omnipotent. And since you are not omnipotent, there is a need for clarity as regards your needs in life. Then, focus on these needs until you achieve them. While I am of the school of thought that supports the act of knowing how to do a lot of things in different fields of life, I am also very aware that you are not meant to do everything. Essentially, any person who tells you they can do everything is either lying or clueless. Identifying a field of play is a major step in getting attention. Identify that field, and focus on it. The Holy Scripture talks about 'this one thing I do'. Look for that 'one thing' you do best and do it in a way no one can ever replicate. When you have done that, people will recognize you for it. Michael Jackson, the black dude turned white is best known for his kind of dance. Today, many years after his death, many people still remember him. You don't need to be good at everything; only in something that leaves an impression in the heart of people. Something they will pay and be grateful for.

One way to dominate any industry is to do what I shared in chapter one which is not to merely take action but to take massive action until you become massive and people call you a 'monster'. Part of the massive action is to out-promote every person in your industry until you instill emotion, anger, and jealousy in the heart of your customers, competitors, and market, respectively. Let your business be first on the mind of your potential customers. Be number one not by making noise, but by providing solutions loud enough that the whole world knows that that is your space. Market your business so loud that the whole world probably hears no one else but you. Think about music in Nigeria for instance, what name comes to your mind? Think about sport, what name comes to your mind? Think about a drink, what name comes to your mind? Think about a friend right now, whose name comes to your mind? Promote! Promote!! Until you are the only name that comes to the mind of people in that particular field. Promote until you have no other thing to do. Promote yourself, your business and products because that is the only way to dominate your space.

ADDED THOUGHTS

The key to success is FOCUS

Focus is the difference between the sun and the moon. The sun is stationary and generates its light with great intensity; the moon, on the other hand, rotates and illuminates less. Focus is critical if you ever want to succeed in business. Your ability to focus on the **mark, price** and **time** is what differentiates you from your competitors.

- Focus on the mark
- Focus on the price
- Focus on the time

1. **Focus on the mark**: Your ability to have a clear cut mark i.e. a goal, a target, a destination is what propels you towards success. The number one secret of success is to have a mark (goal) you wish to achieve and work at it till you achieve it. Knowing the mark also speaks about your

vision. When there is no vision, people live aimlessly. Your ability to have a mark is what markets you to succeed.

2. **Focus on the price**: You have to know how much to pay to get it done. Nobody built an enterprise without first sitting down to count the cost. This speaks about wise planning and programming. Your ability to count the cost for any venture opens you up to know whether you have enough to build or you are just daydreaming.

3. **Focus on the time**: You cannot exist forever. You must calibrate your mark along with time. Have a deadline for all your marks and plans. *'For the vision is for an appointed time'*, not forever. Time must happen for success to have meaning but, remain positive as you work

diligently towards the mark you have set before yourself.

Action taking steps

1. Take a critical look at your business, are you competing or dominating?

2. Write out seven things you can start doing that will help you to leave the circle of competition.

3. In a tabular form, list all the businesses you think you are competing against and categorize them using numbers 1 to 10; where 1-4 means no threat but 5 to 10 means threat. Look for the unique selling proposition of those businesses which are a threat to you; find out what they are doing better than you. Then, come out with strategies that help you dominate that space. (Need help call Dery on 08068387128)

4. What one thing will you do today to improve your life and business from all you have learned in this book? I will recommend that you put it down on paper, and then plan with a deadline for achieving it.